Dash MacIntyre

CABARET NO STARE

2022

Style notes: I find that the capitalization of proper nouns is poetically complex, and the debates I hold in my head about whether capitalizing certain words implies different contexts, intentions, or status to the subjects makes not capitalizing any nouns simpler. It also allows a cleaner read with more concisely consistent spacing between rows of the lowercase text. I exclude the word "I" from this rule, which I keep capitalized not for egotistical emphasis but because stylistically i feel lowercase i's look juvenile and stand out as unnecessary distractions.

Dash MacIntyre has been writing poetry since his college years, and this is a collection of some of his poems spanning the last decade from these chapbooks:

Window Lamp	(2010-2012)
Porch Couch	(2012-2014)
Rooftop Toasts	(2015-2016)
Odd Hours	(2016-2017)
Expatriate	(2018-2019)
Mt. Monastic	(2019-2020)
The Conversateur	(2020-2022)

MacIntyre is also the creator of **The Halfway Post**, a digital newspaper of Dadaist graffiti news and satirical comedy that daily makes fun of Donald Trump.

Besides *THP*, MacIntyre has published comedy lots of places, including *McSweeney's Internet Tendency*, *Points In Case*, *Little Old Lady*, *MuddyUm*, and *The Haven*.

To keep up with MacIntyre's daily writing studio, subscribe to his *Substack* newsletter **The Halfway Café**.

DASH MACINTYRE'S BOOKS

POETRY
Cabaret No Stare (2022)
Moon Goon (2023)
Hotel Golden Hours (2024)

POLITICAL SATIRE
Satire In The Trump Years: The Best Of The Halfway Post (2021)
Satire In The Biden Years: The Worst Of The Halfway Post (2025)

Like my writing? Subscribe to my Substack!

TheHalfwayCafe.Substack.com
Linktr.ee/DashMacIntyre

NO
STARING!

Midwest Face

an obese man who called himself bubba
played guitar in the grocery store and took a break to tell me
watching him from the side
about the women he used to date describing them anatomically
and I listened politely and decided
the responsible thing was to tell him it was 2018
and he shouldn't say inside thoughts like those in public anymore
but he changed subjects to music and asked me if I played
and I said I had dabbled in college
and he told me about the bands he had played in
till the conversation took a sharp turn all of a sudden
to a passionate theory on 'the jews' and I changed the subject
and unoffended he veered to his frustration with 'me too' stories
and how he couldn't even compliment women anymore
and I told him I finally agreed with something he said
that he probably was indeed the kind of guy
who shouldn't compliment women anymore
so he asked me about my band again
and cut me off to talk about his a little more
and remarked how patient I was to listen to him yak
and asked me how old I was though he answered himself
guessing I was too old for his daughter just out of high school
and said he'd been looking for a guy with some sense in him for her
and I further nipped his plan explaining I was taken which he agreed
would have been an easier start to his line of questioning
and he began again to explain the anatomy
of one more woman he once took to bed
and I thanked him for playing guitar to us shoppers
told him I had to go and he gave me his musician business card
and told me to never give up on my dreams
and that if I ever needed cocaine he was my guy.
something about my face
and my midwestern mannered calm
encourages such idiosyncrasies everywhere I go.

Everybody Do Your Part

I was somewhere in harlem in the one-hundred-forties
waiting for the white walker sign to let me cross
when I was grabbed by the arm
and found a head nestling into my shoulder and neck
and I pulled out an ear bud and heard the aggressive heckling
of licentious things about her body
and she looked back and told him
my boyfriend will beat your ass
so I stood up a little taller and looked back
and pointed at him with my finger
and he stopped and walked back the other way
muttering about women these days
and as we crossed the street
she made sure he was gone
and she took a left
and I continued on.

Responsibility To The Neighborhood

their apartment is full of plants
"I don't know about it" they say
uncommitted to the growth
it does look nice from the street I say
for passersby
I admired it on my walk up the block
and with your big street-side windows I point out
you do have a responsibility to the neighborhood
and they agree
and take a can and sprinkle the stems with water.

Bookstore Wall Spider

the bookstore wall spider waits in the corner
between the manga and science fiction
with a stack of art books he studies
and tomes of old german full of philosophic diatribes
I'm not surprised he can read
but he never pays for a book
and every day asks for paper and a pencil
to write down isbn numbers
to find cheaper editions online
to the offense of the store owners
who politely listen to him rant
about the merits of objectivist societies
to the other customers who make the mistake
of walking into his corner web.

Familiarity

I can't believe you didn't introduce us she says
and I recall I did forget to do that
since she already knows so much about them
from observing in the social book of faces
and we talk about them all the time
but yes I remember now
they have not ever officially publicly met
so the familiarity of course could not be revealed.

Naive Millennial

I stood under the marble doorway of the art museum's modern wing
surveying attendees on their experiences of a special exhibit
of discovered underwater artifacts from egypt
and one compliant visitor a white male sixty-five-plus some college
forty k to fifty k no kids under eighteen currently at home
insisted upon me his theories
that egyptian culture was inspired and constructed by aliens
you could tell he told me passionately
because pyramids were also built way across the ocean in the andes
and alien technology was the only logical explanation
though my survey was more interested
in whether he had been to the museum's gift shop or the cafe
back on topic he said he hadn't been to the latter
but had been to the former and for the succeeding question
he had not made any purchases because he told me
in between requests for me to write his reason down
the gift shop had no alien-related gifts
I pretended to record his complaint as he blamed the government
and its deep state conspiracy deniers
for the art museum's extraterrestrial omissions
and I listened patiently before offering a calm counter-theory
that maybe multiple cultures had constructed large pyramids
not necessarily because of alien deus ex machina but maybe because
pyramids are a rather rudimentary constructional concept
of stacking rocks up as high as you can
that children everywhere enjoy doing on their own
and it's maybe not therefore surprising over thousands of years
that disparate empires would individually excel
at stacking their piles of rocks splendidly high
and he thought for a moment
considered it
looked me in the eyes
and called me a naive millennial.

Dalai Voma

the other day a baby made direct eye contact with me
and although I was in the middle
of jotting down a twelve-top order across the restaurant
I was transfixed
baby stared like a glassed lake
and crystallized something in my heart
this was a prodigy self-actualized
far ahead of the top percentile
and he stared
and stared
studying me
learning me
understanding me
judging me
pitying me
and loving me
all unblinking
and then threw up all over himself
without a break in his steely resolve
staring at me as his mother picked him up
staring while taxied away across the restaurant
and staring until only the closed bathroom door
broke
our gaze.
world
I have found the staring contest king
reborn and terrestrial once again
and he has a long successful reign ahead of him.

if you are not your own best friend
favorite vice and all-day free day friend
you're low on something.

The Selfie Place

the selfie place buzzes alive
as the town's cool kids come in for the happy hour social
bringing their own photographers
but the influencers aren't doing much drinking
cause you can't get tipsy or sloppy when cameras are on and everywhere
and they dip inside a ball pit of simulated nostalgia
and toss rubber ducks in a porcelain tub
and hold pillow cloud puffs in a blue walled hallway
and sit on mushroom pleated ottomans between vinyl palms
and put on masks and crowns in the mardi gras loft
and sit for motorcycle poses with a desert highway road projection
as a tray of complimentary flutes of california brut for sipping goes around
and I man the bar serving pink nouveau rosé in glass deco goblets
as the gaggle of digital influencers exchange palaver
and trade social handles and follows for turns at blowing kisses
to politely reciprocated shutter clicks
and a girl in a sweater that says champagne please
turns me down when I offer her some
and another in a mismatch of cougar print and zebra stripes
takes two but they're not for drinking
and she poses in several contortions pretending to enjoy the bubbly
and then gives them back
she can't have them in consecutive photo-ops
and it saliently dawns on me
this is not my kind of night out.

Instagram

concupiscence strikes the affluent nympholeptics
and the pretty girls savvy at branding themselves
conquer the market with their veblen talents.

Jealousless Friends

your most supportive friends will not
be your childhood schoolmates comparing lives forever
but the kindred souls you'll meet briefly
and follow mutually online for the rest of your lives
met mirthfully in little adventures
with fond memories of that one time when...

Orvieto

he had been to orvieto and drank its wine
with a different woman
a previous woman
and when the liquor store promo tasting girl
offered him an ounce of a new brand's orvieto chianti
he swirled it in his mouth and submerged his teeth in it
and let it soak into his tongue and gums
and he got stuck a moment in nostalgia longing for her
the girl he had met in rome
and brought along through umbria decades ago
and the bottles they had shared over several weeks
so he paid the sampler girl a tip
and took three of her orvieto commission bottles
to drink at home and long some more.

Laryangel

she moves her hair
exposes her neck
she's looking me right in the eyes
I'm looking her right in the eyes too
her eyes are nice
I think she's interested
I'm very interested
she's smiling a lot
I'm extra smooth tonight
I keep her laughing and she's shining with a halo
the color of a bright summer cloudless sky
and she moves her hair again to the other side nice nice
this side of her neck is lovely too
I have a laryangel in my midst
her neck is sexy
why are necks sexy
and why do women instinctively show them off
and she's sure showing
she has a sweet voice too
asking me about myself a lot of questions
and I plumb her celestial genesis
this could really go somewhere
she's smiling more I'm smiling most
and she's touching me when she laughs
big laughs now
and she grabs my arm
and squeezes
alright...

Starry Night Over the Rhône

I am not ready to take off my shoes
it is such a semi-drunken night
that I wish upon these stars
I could go out with you
and drink some drops more
in a bar we've never been to
with strangers we won't notice at all
drops which would be perhaps
too much by a bottle
and watch you tell me stories
with your big glittering opulent eyes
and virtuoso flips of your hair
I'd pursue around your shoulders
to the end of the earth.

Young Lady

the old man's face was leathery and creased
with decades of living etched and time tagged
and he gave credit to the carbon monoxide
from the grill coating fossil fuel smoke on his gyro meat
and the ouzo liver scars and lung smears
tarred from his morning cigars
and lunch cigars and dinner cigars
and what are you gonna do about it he asked himself smiling
thinking of his wife who every night used a series of creams
and never drank and never smoked
and still got old alongside him
but of course he never told her that
and always called her young lady.

Oracles

I sat under an olive tree
thinking about morbid disappointments in life
and a man in a fishing vest amidst the tourists
approached me and either asked me
where the acropolis was or if I had been up there
in a difficult italian accent
and I said yes and he accepted the answer
and asked me where I was from and I said st. louis
and he asked where and I said america
and he asked where in america and I said st. louis
and he lied and said he knew it
and I thought maybe here it was
an olive grove epiphany
to turn my dumpster inspirations around
so I listened closely
as he told me about the trips he used to take
to sacramento and san bernardino where his aunts lived
he was very close with his aunts he said
very close in their hearts
and he would fly into jack kennedy
and fly seven hours to the west coast
cause airplanes used to take longer then he said
and now he lived in dubai but missed his native italy
and he asked if I lived here in greece
and I said no my friends do and I get to visit every year
and he said I was lucky and I agreed
and he bid me ciao and left
and I thought to myself what a zen reminder
and then a little bird landed next to me
hopped a bit and flew right past my face so I flinched
and it landed some feet away and hopped some more
to a dead mouse I hadn't noticed in the grass
and flew away with it somewhere else.

For Granted

remember
when life has been a series of conveniences for you
that it could just as undeservedly be
nothing but defenestrations and falling down stairs.

Everywhere Yellow In The Hot August Sun

everywhere yellow in the hot august sun
the sky did not bother fetching any blue today
and won't tomorrow.

the devil is everywhere here
where gnats are kings
in the barren fields of this driest month of a thirsty year.

doldrum molecules slap our faces weakly
few and far between in anemic mockery
of our village's lethargy lazy like the hazy sizzling afternoon.

the bartender pours another glass and I tip a dollar in his jar
the tap pours freely for the village
complimentary to the communal suffering.

nothing to do but drink cervezas
soft and cold and hydrationally dishonest
as sweat drips down foreheads and bottles.

an overhead fan slowly turns.
as we wait for the drought to tire of our valley
we might as well be buzzed.

door to door kidney salesmen inquire
about your weekend habits:
do you recover from binges like you used to
or do you think it's time for a new model?

The Bandaged Bandit

a bearded man matching a composite sketch was detained
for suspicion of a serial string of robberies and murders
going back at least fifteen years
but as he took their questions
the cops noticed his bandaged arm
from a red cross blood donation earlier in the day
and concluded a man so thoughtful about society
could not likely be that day's perpetrator
of such gruesome carnage and fury as they found
and he was released
though the bearded man was in fact the killer
he just happened to know
the importance of donating blood and
as he always reasoned
it left more people alive to kill.
he killed several more times that week
thoroughly devolving in his madness
before the police again obtained him
but he also had been saving three people's lives
every two months or so for two decades as a recurring donor.

Vampiric Friends

I give my blood to them and they call me weekly if I don't
I'm o negative the universal donor
which makes me lots of vampiric friends
but my heart rate doesn't rush the contribution
and keeps me in the donating chair
with the nurses wiggling the needle in my vein
to make it flow a bit faster
so it doesn't pass the regulational limit
and what I've offered already in the rocking bag isn't wasted
but my heart is not a gusher
and they wiggle it one more time and it hurts
while other donors get needled in after me
and leave me still beating slowly
so I lean back and spy the cable television
flashing news stories of the country falling apart
with ticker line reminders of the other countries crumbling too
and I wonder if maybe I shouldn't just give it all away
the rest of my blood
so I don't have to deal with this century anymore
but I think to myself the people I'd save
watching the same depressing stories of civic decay
would not appreciate my donation
or consider it a blessing.

Le Damn

I wandered the catacombs of paris and thought
of all the self-important people
from the middle ages to the 1830s
who would have hated the city's practicality
digging up their ornate graves to move the bones deeper underground
and the anonymity of macabre subterranean decor.

White Flighters

...but now they wanna be cool again
so they go back to the city
but the riffraff is still there so they gotta move in slow
one neighborhood at a time the gentlemen return
gentrifying conquistadors
with faux indifference and plaid shrugs
a few at first with authentic crime rate risk
and cheap housing forgotten by the metropolitan purse
till others see it's not so bad
charming even
and the coffee chains grasp hands
and social mathematics take over
till the area is cliché and everyone tries too hard
and getting dressed takes too long
and parties of people circus about
trying out various personalities
as they mingle conversations in their product placement lives.

Break Out Into Heart-To-Heart Committee Meetings

the party was going swimmingly
but everybody drank a little too much
so things got damp and heavy
and before long family heirloom scars turned pink
as wine tears rolled down cheeks
and exhalations hung up secrets on the laundry lines
till couch dreams arrived and put to sleep the drunks
so their haunts could heal with another passing day.

Kerosene

I had lunch with a dead person today
kerouac on a transient day both hitching into town
and we both missed lunch with separate excuses
that couldn't upset our introverted buccaneerings
and we rescheduled for the night
and met up at an easy bar
and then a pool bar
and a dive bar
and crashed an uptight bar
all the time accumulating traveling wilbury bar rowdies
ready to be alive
so we pulled our new social strings and commandeered
a new friend's apartment up the red train and three blocks
for a found-art friends afterparty spilling out onto the sidewalk
and growing still from errand pedestrians always new friends
with rounds of dumb boasts and oathing sweet toasts
giving all that we could give them
and at six our apartment friends began to stumble away
and we chugged the last beers
as a blue sky sunrise rewarded our sovereign libations
with a golden credits roll of last night's laughs
and the morning joggers and early employees materialized
a little frantic with their coffee commutes
and scowls of jealous pomposity as we cleaned
up the yard strewn cans and closed down the stone stoop's open bar
and smoked the last joint as the city opened for business
and we took one last shot
of whatever discount tequila had been cheapest
at the liquor store on our merry jaunt across town
in honor of the knack for stirring a good night out of thin air
to live the most out of our years even if it costs a few
wherever at the end of the line.

Acetate Reunion

acetate photographs are burning on my heart tonight
and the memory room has a vault door askew
full of faces and colored lights and party cups
on panoramic saturday nights a decade ago
as kid adults practiced independent life
and they're all now older and spread around the country
doing new things with new people in goodbye trajectories
novel organisms with all new replaced cells
my polaroid friends no longer exist
and I have only these chemical flashes of social lightning strikes
and my eyelids droop as the night goes on
and the atomic sketch fades a bit more
and the vault door creaks another inch to shut
and the panoramic people get blurrier and blurrier.

Milieu

the goal of the artist is to direct her own milieu
but only her milieu
the future matters little in the doldrum decades of tomorrow
but if she jams her epochal jazz with a dancing enough groove
and doses of universal honesty
future generations will have her
to contemporize as they need.

I stayed up all night feeling like a bard
crafting a dozen poems I liked
and woke up in the morning to find
there had been fool's gold in my gibberish.

Incumbent

the autumn moon is massive tonight
straight ahead and leading cars east on the interstate
and the fields on each side are vivid with its glow
it must be running for the sun's office of administration
and I have a mind to vote against the incumbent.

November 2016

the election made me a crooner
I have nothing to say specifically
it would take much too long to explain
everything that has gone wrong and unidealistic
the necessary taxi ride would be prohibitively expensive
so crooning is all I got
and I sing from my throat the garbled karaoke tunes
one bar to the next deep into the night
for small drunken audiences whose loners keep stopping me
to tell me to keep singing
loudly in my ear too close with their beer breath
they say it makes them feel a little better.

Catholic Guilt

all the dogma and pomp are nice of course
but catholicism really simply boils down
to the guilt of hourly chiming church bells
interrupting you momentarily in your sinning.

Blood Moon

the late november mourning moon
inhales the last orange and red from the leaves
rising in the vacant purple corpse sky
smoldering with the last of autumn's vigor in a final horizon fire
before mortuary inundation submerges her pallid face
and her subjects offer frost in tribute to the cold.

Raccoon Future

just think that at any moment
some bacteria inside of you could mutate in such a way
that you die
and all the people around you die
and all of humanity gets the game over screen
and the raccoons
or maybe the otters or cockroaches
a dozen million years of evolution later
will get their turn running things on a global scale
all because of your homicidal gut flora.
may the raccoons soar ever higher than we did.

in a way
animals were bred by plants to eat their seeds
and defecate them in new places
just passing this on
because it's a delightful ego check
on all our self-righteous specious bragging.

Everything In Life Is Great

an old labrador white around the eyes and mouth
sits in the truck bed listening
to italian opera music at the drive-in movie theatre
not understanding any bit of this routineless night
but his owners are there with him
so everything is great.

For The Goats

hubris the god sits and entertains
loitering olympic goats chewing olive wreaths
with theatrical shows of our human foibles
as we oath ill-conceived preposterous boasts
and he skewers us with bolts of calling our bluff
and the goats lick up spilled wine as they watch and bleat
and our productions never go dark.

Lieutenant In Arkansas

I found god in arkansas driving past
a monumental neo-classical pentecostal church
with massive columns sculpted grand
like marble behemoths of athenian splendor
towering above luxury cars in the parking lot
and god told me the church deserved to burn
and for the columns to fall on those sedans
cause that flock wasn't spending enough
donatable money on the poor
and they really ought to know that's not allowed
so I obliged the lord.

The No Thanks Explanation

"I got super acid waved out only one time
and I talked to god in a crowded room
there was a party going on a little pedestrian
like a book launch party full of editor introverts or something
and I very much stood out like underdressed at a funeral
and god noticed me over his shoulder and took me aside
and told me never take this drug again this is not for you he said
and it sounds crazy but everyone in the room was like a flame outline
not our bodies but our souls or consciousnesses
or whatever form into which we transcend mortal materialism
and then god went back to his previous conversation
just a calm well groomed host wearing a colorful cone party hat
with a mustache and glasses and a fuzzy sweater and a champagne flute
so for an hour I stood awkwardly in a corner by myself
in this otherworldly room I did not belong in
and that's why I can't take lsd again."

Café Couch

I'm sitting on a comfy little sofa in a café
with a fresh cup of coffee and a book of essays
on various interesting artistic subjects I've never looked into
what a pleasant summer morning I'm having here in chicago
with my article for the day already done
and free time to read with no deadline helmets on my head
yet my thoughts are bogged still in the latest climate report
and its damning and pessimistic apocalyptic predictions
with references to the fires in spain and greece and california
and really everywhere this summer
and I find it surreal like time melting desert clocks
how plugged into the doom and gloom I am
and I decide I must stoically rally myself to maybe picking just one
between whether the world is ending or I am having a lovely day.

POTUC

presidents should chill on the porch
straight up hang out
and drink beers with their aides
and the chief of staff would be there
and the illest cabinet members
and a supreme court justice with weed
and just for good measure
a senator in need of a rolling for a vote
and when it gets dark
and the tourists beyond the fence can't tell for sure
they should pass a joint of an experimental strain
rolled by the secretary of agriculture
with cheers clinked to the country and the idealism of the people
celebrating unprecedented policy agreement
and they'd drink a bunch of cans on the lawn til late at night
and leave a twenty dollar tip for each of the groundskeepers
under a handful of gravel rocks on the patio table.

In Memoriam

I want in memoriam
an anonymous statue in a viridescent downtown park
with a nameplate fallen off and lost
or if not that a street named after my forgotten surname
pronounced wrong when directions are given
or if not that a plaque on a bench somewhere I used to sit
that few walkers stop to read
or if not that a picture in a frame of me
stashed in the middle somewhere of a great big landfill.

American Sacrifice

snipers in the windows are trying to make me die for my country
I love the motherland but I do not hate these window men
and I wish we could all go home back to our wives and children
our saturday afternoon hobbies and nightly scotches
and return to our blissful ignorance of each other's existence
but our statesmen have irreconcilable differences
so they send us peaceful people to war
while they go back to their wives and children
their saturday afternoon hobbies and nightly scotches
and other comfortable materialisms
with willful ignorance of other corners of the world
and while pinned down behind a car in front of you
waiting for my folk to advance behind you
I honor your previously comfortable life
your lovely wife's warm body under the covers at night
your angel children reading books on the floor
your finesse with your nightly hobbies and talents
your love for single malts tingling with the day's successes
and your unfamiliarity with me
you couldn't recognize me on the street if I walked past
how beautiful your life is!
unfortunately I am more fond of mine
and I am afraid my folk will have to annihilate you and yours
for me to return home and forget all this
I sincerely hope our mortars are quick and painless
and I truly honor the sacrifice you are making for me.

sundrenched in the morning
waking up to the light through open curtained windows
leaves a soft impression that life can be quite alright.

Legacy

I like to think of myself as a civil war portrait
a striking face with piercing eyes in black and white
lying in a field in the cannon littered mud
dead and sacrificed for the cause
and inserted into a historical documentary film
ignored by texting high school students
in apathetic classrooms of underfunded public schools
on the old side of redlined neighborhood districts.

Modern Jesus

the modern jesus confesses to all the crimes of the year
at the reception desk of the police station
but the prison wardens want their bonuses
and have state reservations full in the books
so they tell jesus to go but he won't
and they arrest him for not resisting arrest.

Thin Blue Line

it's quiet tonight but the arrests pay the bills
so blinding spotlights beam down alleyways and side streets
from marauding justice cars in the neighborhood maze
stalking civil rights in darkened drives
doing the shady things impunity allows
when we don't arrest our own.

Class Warfare

I went to work at 9:30am and worked a double
came home at 11:45pm and went to sleep
went to work at 9:30am and worked a double
and came home at 12:30am
and my third double in a row
included the owner of the restaurant
who had the weekend off like every weekend
coming in and spending on himself
the corporate riches of my triple double labor
and it was my turn to serve him
and he explained to his friends as he sat them down
how much he was worth because of the hard work he did
in his quiet little peaceful office
somewhere far away from this smoky bbq place
and he ordered eight meals for five people
and fifteen drinks a cocktail for each course
and made me not ring any of it up
just tell the bartender and head chef what he wanted
and he took two hours of my dedicated attention
and at the end of the meal he did not have to pay for
he did not tip me
so I murdered him and put his head on a stake
in the flower pot out front of the patio
and the answering police officer was a union man himself
and understood the story I related
so he let me go with a warning
and I went back to serving tables
since mine was a closing shift.

The Bipartisan Compromise

at the restaurant
the bill ticket had a twenty sitting atop it
and the credit card slip had a $0 on the tip line
with a written note in pen taxation is theft
from a libertarian who credit to him
put his money where his mouth was
and the waiter half of me appreciated the gift
of a tax-minded tip off the record
but the socialist half of me regretted the thievery
from the country and its coffers
and both the conservative's call for self-interest
and the liberal's call for civic duty
dueled their moral revolvers but both missed
so after cashing out my last table I resolved
to meet them somewhere about the spectrum middle
and bought some drugs from a dishwasher the restaurant over
and smoked out my fellow waiters and cooks
to trickle down relief a dealing robin hood
for a happy buzz as we wrapped and wiped and swept and mopped
the double shift's end and a hard day's night.

Wasabi Tears

she cried thinking about an empty ocean
after we'd caught all the fish and starved the whales
and boiled and oiled and ate everything else
we murderers of the seas
with centuries of taking and never giving back
or even an odd year of smaller nets or shorter sailing routes
and holding off on new sushi bars in landlocked places.

Americana

in rural small town thrift stores
like fossils of boomer nostalgia
are reagan biographies and religious right memoirs
and a table full of crucifixion statues
and a shelf of clocks with intrusive ticking
and a rack of framed rockwell prints
and coffee cups branded with declining employers
and relocated companies long gone
and gaudy brass lamps and santa figurines
and grandparent denim pants worn and faded in the seat
from sedentary years of sitting on the couch at home
for old television show marathons
and then the car to church
on the pew for the sermon
in the booth at the rustic country buffet
to the café sipping coffee swapping grandchild stories
and back on the couch at home
in time for the evening opinion news.

Civics Lesson

remember kids the first amendment says
the government can't physically shut you up
but nowhere does it say large crowds of people can't
collectively decide you're a dumpster dupe with trash beliefs
and use their free market autonomous rights to boycott
businesses spending advertising money on your programming
to suggest companies not allow their corporate brands
be associated with a dumpster dupe with trash beliefs.

Dearborn

the dumb islamophobic moron watched hours of videos online
every week of the dangers of muslim immigration
so he decided to take a trip to dearborn michigan
and see for himself the burgeoning caliphate
no doubt plotting his murder and his nation's overthrow
so he drove and stopped at a middle eastern grocery
but was surprised to see the shelves in order
and white customer regulars asking for their usuals
and family employees diligently restocking.
hungry from the drive he walked to the deli and ordered a sandwich
and watched to see if they'd sneak a blade in his veggies
but saw no sign of sabotage or other danger
and the cashier smiling at him in her hijab
handed him his sandwich with an unordered bag of chips
and when he looked at her confused
she told him it was on the house and to pay for it forward
for someone else to brighten the day of another of god's children
and to have a great day himself.
the dumbstruck islamophobic moron thought to himself
what a case of bad luck
to walk into what must be the only non-terrorist
middle eastern grocery in all of michigan.

Family Resemblance

gone with the wind
more like embarrassment in the lingering breeze
fuck the southern antebellum
nothing is more undeserved than nostalgic reverence
for wasteland plantation culture pearl clutchers licking
slavery's blood money to distract from how much like pa
all the slave kids look.

Ferguson

the city burns at night
this supermoon season has driven us mad
golden lofted in the air like an attic bedroom light
why does it speak to us through voices in our head
amplifying our doubts and fears wide awake late into the night
contemplating the things we oft ignore in unearned passivity?
it tells us we're alone
and we must act out to prison-escape
it whispers if we are to be caged by demographics
with zoological zeal for city planning we might as well earn it
but lashing out never stops the anguish
it only feeds the negative attention addicts
it is an anger relapse and a step backward
and to the other side of the arc
nonviolence is a decades-long outstretched hand
amidst a status quo of bullets sinking into flesh
a block down from the grand boulevard ritz
and red marker drawn fences on the real estate map
and missing umbrellas of police attention
the status quo is an immobile beach corpse
to be blown to smithereens and picked up as bits of carcass
and in a fire ceremony ringed around together
we must examine the mangled pieces and taste them
and smear the blood of communal failure on our foreheads
and when the behemoth has been sucked dry
we will see the metal skeleton and how the cogs all fit
it was not natural
it was a broken machine from another era
for hierarchal manifest destiny and legislative exclusivity
and attention span suburb gavels tipping the scale
with the cognitive dissonance of "I'm not racist but..."
and white parents who discourage their kids
from playing with black children
in another generation's apprenticeship of segregation.

I'm An Ally

an old morose morbid looking white lady in a motorized scooter
controlled by a grandma-winged arm passed by me in a rural walmart
and pointed out the people of color to me
and said I guess assuming me a teammate
"there's too many n****** around"
so I told her she shouldn't use that word
and she huffed about political correctness baloney
so I said okay
there's too many shit life syndromed bigots like you around
raising up our healthcare costs with trans fat hedonism and cigarettes
and voting in pandering culture war maniacs for the oligarchy
you're what there's too much around of
not some random people just existing with a little more melanin
and she gasped
and opened her mouth to scold me
so I told her to shut her dumb meth mouth
and all its political correctness baloney
and maybe she had an aneurysm or some other malfunction
because she got quiet stammering and babbling things to herself
and I said it looked like she actually quite liked the conveniences
of casual political correctness
and she humphed at me and turned her head
and her scooter slowly motored away.

Rule #1

rule number one:
just try to keep your head in your brains
no your brains in your head
ah I've messed it up already.

29

Celestial Sign

the comet came around every couple centuries or so
big and bright green startling the feudal folk
pondering how its presence up there in the sky
should prophesy upcoming plans of war and siege
and after short deliberations on the heavenly mandate forecast
the king and all his nobles agreed they could not lose
so the knights put on their horses all their ornaments of war
marched out on roads in foreign plains
and when they were all slaughtered fast outnumbered large
the castle's lords filled up cathedral pews
and argued over who knew most
the celestial sign had called for caution.

Dresden

I had not voted for war and instead cried tears for the republic
I never wore the armband or saluted the angry clown
did not raise my arm to troops out in the street
and was saddened to see the little boys and girls grow up wearing stars
but I did not speak out
I took the easiest path worn by the country's feet
and when the sirens came on and the city began to burn
I supposed we deserved it for london and rotterdam
and whatever happened to those jewish children
when the trains took them away
I regretted only that the victorious occupying allies
would not be able to walk our beautiful streets
and see for themselves the architecture and culture
that had inspired our delusions of national grandeur.

Southern Success

black man hanging from an oklahoma tree
because his shoe shop was a success
making more money selling more shoes
than the other shops nearby
and one of the town was brother to the county sheriff
moonlighting in white sheets under dark new moons
and another was a coroner who claimed he looked
and could verify it was an apparent suicide hanging
and the bruises must all have been self-inflicted
so the black man's family moved to a city way up north
with loss of dad and wealth and home
in a crumbling house of a neglected neighborhood
left behind by frightened white folks
and they grew up breathing in a sawmill's dust
and the bitter air of northern poverty
keeping at bay the nightmare of southern success.

Eidolon

the screaming of the sadistically tortured shackled
the keening of the abandoned bereaving orphaned
the aching of the chronically rickety invalided
the anguishing of the depth diving mentally ill
the praying of the desperately yearning and alone
and the tearing of innumerable suffering everywhere
must be like an evening symphony for our omniscient god
who doesn't interrupt the show.

The Thing About Jesus

the thing about jesus is that he's billed as the savior
of all mankind because he died on a cross
as if it were some ultimately painful death in sacrifice for our sins
but let's be honest
being crucified as far as punishments go isn't really that bad
like for sure it sucks but
there are much more memorable ways to suffer
like prometheus of another mythology
chained to a mountain and every single day
an eagle comes and tears out his organs with its beak
and it has been happening for thousands of years
and it happened today and yesterday and all throughout the 80s
and will happen tomorrow and the day after and so on forever.
in fact
to hype up jesus's measly crucifixion from town to town in every land
is merely unimaginative in that ancient empire
and his suffering only lasted several hours
which as far as historical crucifixions go
is not much to create a christ around
ahead of most condemned roman victims
hanging from their nails for days parching in the hot sun.
beyond wood beams humans have invented much worse
like cooking each other in bronze bulls
where the metal burns add insult to injury
as your screams make music from a built-in horn
so your death entertains your torturers
as they sip their digestifs in the king's banquet hall.
being strangled is a crazy way to go out
maybe it's shorter but talk about an aggressive way
for jesus to die rolling on the ground being strangled
by judas for ten amateur minutes until jesus passes out
and maybe gets his face and skull stomped on.
or being drawn and quartered torn to pieces for royal offense
which wasn't a very cheek-turning thing for medieval christians to do.

or wasting away through months of auschwitz medical torture
losing his mind starving on wooden planks
with a bucket of bad water and black bread to accompany
his lice and typhus until he wastes away and is tossed into a furnace.
or being chased through swampy woods for a week by dogs
and beat and lynched for talking to a white woman.
or drafting into a pointless and unwinnable war in a country
whose independence his occupation efforts are betraying.
or growing pale and weak denied health insurance claims
thanks to a preexisting condition and maxed out lifetime care
with no miracles from pharma executives browsing yacht magazines.
or getting captured and detained for years
as a desert sex slave and beheaded on live television.
or being chopped into pieces by a fossil fuel dictator
and shrugged off and ignored by arms dealers.
what if jesus had died of starvation
slowly on a cold street in a town whose charitable impulses
got banned by civic laws criminalizing charity?
I guess I don't know what I'm trying to get at
but perhaps we fetishize the suffering of our prophets
to ignore the suffering of the living.

I Do Not Personify The Numinous

a girl in college who didn't know me very well
once developed a crush on me
and felt so strongly she exclaimed
she could feel god was bringing us together
to share in union our mutual love for jesus christ
and couldn't I feel it too?

The Absurd

there are times where the lives of my other universe selves
seem arranged like standing dominoes
drawn in a flipbook shown in a kinetoscope peephole
backwards and forwards in a tunnel of space and time
and I see the stepping stone moments of all my universe bubbles
I am a few billion linear seconds on a planet moving fast
in circles around a sun moving even faster
and I exist always and existence is a ruse
fooled with chemicals into thinking I have agency
with specified cells turning ocular tricks
seeing things upside down and fixing it in post.

Tooth

a man I met from deep down south
where the water doesn't move
has kept a tooth for years in his mouth
and when he eats he takes it out
sets it on the table next to his glass of vermouth
and when he's finished and wipes his lips with a napkin
he puts the tooth back in for good luck he says
knocking three times on the gnarled table top
cause back when that molar was snug inside his gums
things were going pretty well.

the uniformly dressed looked around
at the dictatorship gotten out of hand
regretting finally what they've done only after
staring into their comrades' firing squad rifle tips.

Rooftop Toast

the world's media erupts into the viral sensationalism
of the earth's impending annihilation:
the space nations' satellites unanimously confirm
a moon-sized asteroid is a half hour away
and I'm up on my roof in a lawn chair
with a tall glass of bourbon
watching the world struggle to poorly accept
its momentous end.

The Binge

I found salvation
in a three am fast food burger
but salvation did not sit well
in the night's deluge of devil water
and I threw god up.

N95

"be the light" says her shirt
the woman in the grocery store screaming
at a high school aged front door employee
reminding her the store pandemic policy is to wear a mask.

Self-Portrait #9

I am old wine left in a glass on the nightstand
molding on top with putrid scents
wraithly emanating throughout the room
like a little hint of the debt to death
someone must pour me out
wash the cup and open the window to freshen the air
and spray a bottle themed on fresh linen.

Smile From The Casket

I went to the dentist for the first time in years
confessing only to one
and the dentist marveled at my teeth
for not looking at all as if it had been so long
and I can lie to my dentist
but the rest of my genealogical tree branches
whisper of an early heart attack
so someone at my funeral please
stick a finger in my lips and pinch a cheek up
to show off my dental vigor
to all my mourning friends.

the mistakes I've made
are too many for a film
and now are collected in a span of seasons
for binging in home theaters.

Tousled Gyri

the sun is setting gold in the leaves
and I'm unsettled or dissettled or missettled
I don't know which
and I don't know what I want
I don't know that I want anything
I have what I used to want
I'm not missing anything
but I'm low and down and the sky is purple
and the hot day is cooling at last...
maybe I'm asettled
nah that's not it either
but I just want to continue being alone
thinking disheveled thoughts in my tousled gyri.

she was my summer cicada
and left me in about the same manner.

Headlights In The Puddles

where do people drive off to at 12:49
on a late tuesday evening after a tempestuous thunderstorm
whose petrichor still haunts the surfaced worms
beneath lingering misty fogs above the pavement
sprayed out from underneath the night owls' truck tires?

Midnight Drinkers Of The Moon

something's bubbling in my veins
my arms are getting numb
and my legs are getting jazzy
and I'm tapping on the desk with spider fingers
moving to a rhythm faster than the one I'm stuck in
I need a ride to a new city
to peak around in neighborhood bars
and find the midnight drinkers of the moon
who haven't any intentions of falling asleep.

Dad Is The Boss Of Grandpa's Company

somewhere a rich trust fund baby executive
is kneeling in the bathroom on his knees
snorting coke off a toilet tank cover truant from a meeting
because he got too stoned at lunch and can't go in there yet
with his glossy red intergalactic eyes
so he jerks off into the bowl to googled nudity on his phone
with a music playlist streaming bob marley out loud
and no consequences will come to him this decade.

here's a little ode to the little last morsels
that groups of professional women leave behind
on plates in the restaurant
cause they don't ever want to be seen in public
suggesting an unsatiated appetite
finishing every bite.

Musa Paradisiaca

every morning a banana half was waiting
for years and decades half eaten
half saved for him when he woke up
sitting on the top fridge shelf to cut and add to his cereal
until she died and he had to eat her half too
whole bananas each morning from then on
as he thought of memories in memoriam
and meditated with relief
he didn't have much longer either.

Purple

the coals smoke into the purple summer sky
as the chicken is lathered with olive oil
dripping in the briquettes and sprinkled
with oregano and garlic and the grill top is placed
and the paleo smell wafts out the little air vents
and the moon rises above the trees full and white
and the fireflies come out blinking their yellow lanterns
and the sky turns dark and the chicken turns brown
and finally it's time to eat.

The Asteroid Galaxy Tour

after the daylight lie in the garden
to watch the sky flicker and dance its celestial choreography
of planets juggling moons and spinning rings and introducing
traveling asteroids sticking around a week or two
performing touring vaudeville shows with jokes and parodies
of the cosmic things going on elsewhere in the galaxy.

Prayer In Nature's Palm

at ten o five I am the only one in my building
and on my street outside
on my second story balcony
with a view of all the backyards
the only one not at work
yet
and the late february sun shines on my bare pale chest
and shoulders and weak arms
cooking out the juices of this late winter common cold
as I listen with my eyes closed to all the sun streaks through the trees
while squirrels run down power lines
and the birds braving from their nests
are a wonderful few minutes of peace the universe of atoms
has arranged exclusively for me
and now it's ten-thirteen
and I have to go in to get ready at ten-twenty
to leave on time at ten-thirty
to cut it close and get to work by eleven...
seven minutes left
of this february twenty-fifth's morning gold.

Not That This Is That, But

the worth in reading poetry
is every once in a while you find a sentence
or a thought or a metaphor
that just sucker punches your attention
and you remember here and there
and think it to yourself
for the rest of your enlightened life.

Resolutions

december unwraps the optimism of an annual year review
followed by an ambitious preview of the coming twelve months
and you decide this year will be different
and you'll early get a bit ahead
in all your goals and lofty hopes
and you sign your pen on the dotted line contract
and rush out of the office excited
before you sit and do the math a bit deeper
and see you've been unfortunately
unrealistically sold.

don't read the bible
compile your own
it will make a lot more sense
teach you much more about contemporary society
and generate brighter electricity at dinner parties.

The Poet's Fear

I write write write must write everything
all that comes to me with obsessive compulsion
and not slow myself down with questions of whether it is right
just singularly accept that it all must be written
for better or for worse
and hope that the consensus
from the audience at large of my mausoleum words
is not that I'm deranged.

Wear Your Galoshes

I'm a bad omen son of rain
on a morning of gold and then cloudless blue
before the menace squall swept in amused it was late
and pushed the early flirting spring out of bully winter's way
and the little buds in their dents in the ground
hunched their backs and waited out the rain
and sleet and finally a fusillade of hail
for a march spring thaw only after my newborn cries ceased.

Pluviophile

easter clouds have splashes of grey in their white puffs
and the drizzling rain unleashes the aromas of the earth
like it does the oils of whiskey in my glass
and the afternoon drops puddle ponds on the street
and showers the dusty lawn of long grass
and sprinkles my feet and legs to my knees
as I sit on the porch and read
and in an hour the neighborhood front lawn fields
are their most verdant of the year
and I wonder if in the idea
of the common conception of heaven
would I be allowed to sit out on a patio
listening to birds and dripping roof gutters on a rainy april day
and read good writing to myself sipping a glass of scotch
and would god leave me alone?

New Tenant

in early march I found a bird had made its nest
in the bush beside my front door
under the roof of my patio overhang
so I knocked on the nest and demanded it start paying rent
twenty worms a week.

Revolution Of The Bipedal Prairie

the trees are all arrested and sentenced
for standing in the way of sprawling progress
and chainsaw guillotines do their justice
while the revolution of the bipedal prairie
allows some slaves for neighborhood shade
and to not make hypocrites of all the avenues
named elm and maple birch and oak.

at cannae
and changping
and austerlitz
and gettysburg
and ypres
and stalingrad
the grass gets back to work.

April

hail fists pound on the window panes
and she paints and paints in brushes on white
all the basking glimpses she's caught on fairer days
of daffodils and amaryllis and green grass in the cement cracks
and blue jays in bushes and bunnies munching daisy bunches
till she conquers the precipitation
and the sun lets loose again its gold in honor of her portraiture
and she earns her nap in the hammock out back
for never letting rain get her down.

Little Tabitha Rasa

putting my grocery items in the bag
at the counter past the checkout
I see a little baby girl sitting in a cart
looking curious at me innocently
laboring to find sense in me
developing into consciousness right there
grappling with riddle answers to the mysteries of life
based indispensably on my funny face
so look all you want little villager study me all you like
I'll even make you giggle with a facial contortion
everyone in society has a village responsibility
to make the babies smile.

"I don't want to have kids
cause I know I'd get all girls
because of how shitty I've treated them my whole life..."

Sargasso Creep

he was an eel from the depths of atlantic mystery
and swam through the rivers of new england
and down into a mississippi bar
where he kissed her in the face
and grabbed her breasts
waiting in the hallway for respective bathrooms
and she punched him in the ear
stomped on his toes
kicked him in the nuts
and found his grandmother and mother online
and told on him
so he'd soon get beat again.

Monday Morning Stories

she has too many friends who tell the same stories differently
to different people
their inconsistent narcissism is a peacocking game
she's bored playing with its submissive shrugs
of assertive self-deprecation over alleged flaws
standing tall as pillars of vanity mimicking manic egos
who hate to be at home alone with slideshow recap disappointments
projected on the walls of their deep dark skullery
with sizzling bulbs of missing-out fears illuminating amateur arts of self
with truthful skins carpet-rolled off suburb river bridges
to calm shaky hands and restless feet en route to friday nights downtown
anxious for flinging social pennies with false start laughs and trying too hard
hanging up gaudy decor ribbons of impulsive bar tab receipts
to have their names included in the lunchroom table talk
of all the weekend stories monday morning.

The Merch Store

the live event merch store is a melee of triple xl shirt requests
but all we have is up to two xl
so dads and boyfriends and husbands don't fit
and the women's sizes run about two sizes small
so most women don't fit either
but they all want to try the two xl size
even though we told them they run small
and we comply to each request
there's just no polite way to say
I've been here all day and I can tell already looking at you
you're too big
so we go to the bin and get a double xl
and when they hold the shirt against their chests
and stretch the neck up to their chin
and pull the bottom down toward their hips
it doesn't quite reach not even close
so they give it back and we have to refold it
and put it back into the bin
and come back to the next person in line
who from experience I can see won't fit into any of our shirts
but they have to see it for themselves.

Whose Walk Is This?

the walk is interrupted by the humans off their leash
and I sit and wait for my owners to gab
patiently sniffing the neighborhood scents
eyeing the interruption going a little long
it's my walk not theirs.

Afraid Of The Vet

his eyes hang low afraid
though comforted by us around him
but it's a false security
we are not there to pull him through
not this time
and they put the needle in his leg ready for our cue
to flood his heart with the end
and we grab his paws one last time
kiss him on his head and rub his soft ears
nod
and he doesn't fade away
so much as in a second turn still
and tears come for the fifteen years he gave us
of laughs and amusement
and all the charming facets of his domestication.

Heat & Hum

you reminisce about the summer as it gets close
somewhere in mid march
the heat and hum of insect multitudes
and whirling air conditioner fans
somehow always turning on just as you walk past
and firefly dusks when it's cool enough to be out
and when the first heat wave settles in for the week
a couple new moons or so later
one hundred and more for six straight days
you are reminded of winter months and snow
cold and quiet with sweaters and jeans
boots and backyard fires from somewhere in your nose
and you start sneaking peaks at the colder looking pictures
a few calendar pages ahead.

Highway Glow

a lightning bug on an evening jaunt
crossed into my highway lane and exploded on my windshield
leaving green juices glowing in the dark
for a minute till it faded dark and dry.

Little Green Stems

the inspirations of winter escape from the struggle against it
its cold its chill its wind its snow
and the village locks arms and tightens hunched backs
melting palms to trash can fires
in cabins surrounded by the plains' sharp chill
whistling its dusk time howl of the great arctic wind
on its january prowl down from the glacial north
while the villagers kill time inside for the months of frost
till the latitude thaws and the ice recedes
and little green stems reach boldly for the sun
beckoning warmth back to the hemisphere.

Evening Stroll

when it gets dark enough to justify an illuminant
hold out for half an hour longer
and get weird in that dusky living room darkness
and soak up the emptiness
and saturate the melancholy
as the rest of the neighborhood electrifies their bulbs
to keep their demons and ghosts away
up in the tall far ceiling corners
then go take yours out for a stroll.

The Metropolis Across The River

her list of all the girls she had ever shared love
was an underwhelming notebook page
but the metropolis across the river
called out fantasies on boring weekend nights at home
and sang back when she howled out her loneliness
and she cracked her piggy bank
escaped the suburb and found some roommates
and got to scribbling in that lovers notebook
and when she returned on a hometown weekend
her family and friends found this quiet girl's shell removed
and the big city's millions had allowed anonymity enough
to finally be herself.

Dumping Of A Muse

the greatest artistic fissure is a dumping of a muse
she just matured that's all it was
and he replaced her with a smoother more taut porcelain doll
to lie across the divan and nourish impressionist oeuvres
as many as can trace her curves
before he spits her too out like a sucked seed
salivating with both anguish and elation for the novel blank ephemeral stares
of always new indifferent young women missing father molds
pursuing paternity from his easy nightstand money
as he coaxed out opuses onto immortal canvases
with lustful hues across provocative compositions
painting the summer's ambitions for them both
those august days of the early 1880s that live forever in museum frames.

Phryne On The Dance Floor

she did not mind a select guy here and there
touching her in the middle of the late night clubs
knowing time was not kind to curves like hers
and she wanted them all to remember
the august femininity her twenties
had gifted to the world.

Eros Borealis

the pearls in her eyelashes stared deep
enough to sear my outside cardiac tendons
and she met me at juicy medium rare
as she gave me little gifts of bottled up jars of eros borealis
to take out at night and spread across the ceiling
at the end of my bedtime routine.

Patriarchal Princes

fuck boy is an apt feminist critique of male patriarchy
and its grown up princes with ironic oedipal hangups
and coddled fragile states of mind
degrading women with self-conscious impotence
from inability to return the social favor of orgasm
as they self-consciously make up for shallow dives
with choleric quantity.

Pisces

a sun too big for its own good
the fusion engines drain and dry greasy
in between flash flooding fission bursts
from visions of women I'd love to love
over-irrigating ventricles flaring out plasma rings
everyone put on your sunglasses
I get no rest it never ends
when one glows dim at the edge of the event horizon
another dusty cloud plunges in and I'm burning up again.

Flower Dresses

a lovely girl wore flower dresses every day
even when it rained
and that's what nourished my attraction
but I broke up with her for another lovely girl
who only wore flower dresses on sunny days
and my first musing lady stopped wearing them all together
and the second didn't work out either
and gave up too those floral reminders
of incomprehensible me
who loved those dresses so much.
subtracting two pretty girls dressed in daisies
carnations orchids marigolds petunias and calla lilies
this is my apology to the world for darkening it just a little
because I was not yet the man the darlings deserved
and it's a misfortune for girls they mature much faster.

Love What I Can Give You... While I Have It

we all worship the culture of love boasting total immersion
that part is easy
easy for fresh minted passion taking us where it does
unilingual and shades of colors you've never seen
without brunette tickles in your nose
while the screen plays tragedies irrelevant to your novel
a kaleidoscope of lasting archaic trust
but the honey-I'm-home kiss batteries run out
and the sex gets unplugged
boxed up and stored for the next hallmarked holiday
loveless marriage is now our national pastime
while our distinct species of butterflies go extinct
lost in empty opaque smiles.
the course may never run smooth
but shakes never admitted that the course is finite
that the divorce courts lick their lips while the cake is cut
commitment is hard
staying in shape is hard
having kids is hard
following through on anything is hard
I get it
I understand why we give up.
when you climb to the top of the mountain
the journey only leads downhill
back to the skepticism of an existential paradise
you can no longer hallucinate in the denser oxygen of reality
and my heart has never been surefooted
tumbling down quick at the first
short
breath.
so sorry sweetheart
that we can't conquer hubris
but love what I can give you...
while I have it.

Egotistical Delirium

you get home and think about it alone in the basement
under a single incandescent light bulb
in a corner of broken glass playing your guitar to cockroaches
and empty parking lots outside
buried in snow up to the precipice of your piscean sanity
as the end of the night envelopes you into a womb
with blanketing amplification of electric romantic relapse
from emotional and alcoholic sobriety
while your hole in the ground spins like a top
and cardiac delusions flitter about
as absinthine sprites mock and laugh at you
because you were in love and she was not.
a string snaps and it reminds you're too intoxicated
to stand let alone pretend you're capable of music
and you crumble to the floor and stare at the ceiling wooden rafters
feeling sucker punches from the universe itself
deep in your psyche with its merciless chemical taunts
and you melt with spatial and pathos meaninglessness
into the square of carpet like a raft in a sea of cold cracked concrete.
laughing itself out the light bulb flickers and shatters in a bang
of meteor glass and ringing tinnitus beneath blue holiday lights
stars stranded heavenly across suspended leaded cords
as your quiet appeals for the galaxy's electrons to treat you kinder
are muffled by heavy snowflakes outside
indifferent to your ego crisis in this heartless february witching hour
while the liquor waves pounce and splash until at long last
the concrete calms and your upset mind turns placid
and the flames in your eyes dim
with the last of the day's battered consciousness
and the blue stars wander deep into your tributary veins
and a black vignette cradles your head to drift you off to sleep
humming soft lullaby prophesies of a bright morning soon
whispering finally its tenderest reminder:
who the fuck cares?

Desert's Teachings

in a dream of emancipated aviator ghouls
dogfighting over ghost town casinos in the desert
he was shot down into the desolate sand
between mountains of red rock on every side
and found a shrub with gifts of kaleidoscopic hallucinations
when he burned it keeping warm at night
and interpreting its galaxial prophesies
he swore rousing inner oaths to a bright ecclesiastic comet
in the nightly milk mentoring his catechisms
as he tuned his homiletics with curious lizards
and mastered over many months his cosmic metaphysics
and finally found himself one morning in his hometown in his bed
it had only been a dream but as the day went on
still the desolate visions seared vividly the walls in his skull
with metaphors and moral tales and ontological ruminations
of solipsistic transcendence and novel epistemological premises
and he kept them there unvoiced and unheard for years
till the moment would be right when the comet's green arrived
and the people of the material realm now almost but not yet
would be ready for the desert's teachings.

Whew

he awoke in the middle of the night to find his entire body numb
and immovable save his crisis surveying eyes
no arm control nor wiggling toes
so he stared at the ceiling wondering about permanence
and decided if it was for real
he'd worry about it in the morning
and he closed his eyes back to sleep
and was thankful when he woke up
the sleep paralysis was gone.

Cultural Immersion

I was reading in my bed for existentialism class
when the guys from honduras costa rica and colombia
invited me to their dorm suite for a smoke
where they rolled a week's worth of herb in a preposterous joint
passed it around the circle five times three indulgent hits each stop
and called each other gay in different spanish ways
over and over and laughed till it hurt
and tears streamed down their pinkened faces
and they took turns explaining to me in english
why their insults were so funny
and within the genre there were a few masterpieces
and when the joint was done they leaned back
on the dorm's two twin beds and two corner recliners
and fell deeply asleep with me alone awake
wondering what I should now do
all in thirty minutes' time
so I left their room back to mine back into bed
and continued on in the existentialist books.

Artistic Purity

is there any art more artistically pure
than the graffiti scrawled anonymously
in the pages of marriott hotel mormon bibles
done neither for money nor recognition
and possibly paying the price of a soul
to leave a little divertissement flair?

First Amendment

the poet only wrote odes to the sensation of excrement
violently pushing through his colorectal exit
some three thousand works over the course of several years
twice or thrice daily with vivid metaphors and similes
some lasting dozens of stanzas in creative formats
with blasphemous biblical symbolism
and unexpected references to canonical literary classics
and he self-published his work in a towering tome
covered with a vulgar print of goatse in pop pulp comics style
he printed himself at great cost
delivered to his home in bulk on a pallet every month
and he snuck in copies at bookstores to leave on every genre's shelf
and planted copies in as many thrift stores
and school libraries as was geographically practical
until infamous
and eventually legislatively censored
convincingly quite unconstitutionally
by his city then his state then the country
in vehement trials of unredeeming indecency on all sides
and
well...
he could have branched out a bit.

he went to the art museum with a brush and some paints
but got arrested soon after
and it took the police several hours to confirm
he really was the artist signed to the tampered canvases
just a perfectionist unable to rest
while a conspicuous absence of necessary brush strokes
continued to leave his impressions incomplete.

Santa's Book

the mall santa loved his job getting paid to sit and be cheery
and light up children's december days
as the prize of their long line calendar wait
stepping up to their christmas hero
climbing into his lap and whispering in his ear
the one thing they wanted most that year
and he was so good at it
gaining weight at the start of every september
maintaining a snow white curly beard
and practicing his ho ho ho's
and the parents all loved him
and the mall asked him annually to return in his cap and boots
and he wondered what could be more fulfilling
than the gap-toothed smiles and stoked ideas of magic
full of childish innocence he respected so much
until he read lolita
and the thoughts it enkindled did not forget themselves.

Laudanum Ladies

me and the neighboring housewives
idling in the 1890s noon
but only I am under the influence
or am I alone
should I check in with them
maybe they have harder drugs
probably
cooped up every day
I would.

Derailed

the day is over
a day that derailed my life
my eyes on the tumbler
a swishing of the rocks
swallow it all
my alcohol doll
and no more rocks
straight scotch shots
waste all my money
and fall on the floor
get kicked out the door
fuck this fuck them
there's throw-up in the urinal
and urine in the alley.

Petard

there have been a few magical intuitions
in my short and fungal life
in which momentarily I was absolutely sure
the universe was looking out for me specifically and significantly
with gravity waves emanating deep from in my core
as if I was some root of destiny idealistic and without falling over
weathering all that is blown at me
but then it's never long after
before I hoist myself spectacularly
again with my own petard.

One For The Team

I have a feeling of a censorship ultimatum
not of a ripped out tongue or cut hands or exile from wifi
but exhilarating assassination
I will challenge someone heavy proving them so wrong
in such a delusion-threatening way
I'll convince them not of my cause or specific frame of view
but of a persuasion I should not be permitted
with my progressive ideas and dangerous charm to exist at all
but wouldn't I be a bohemian flower and democratic weed
if my humanistic passions struck with projectile infamy
murdered for my particular brand of existentialism
beckoned some iconography for the trendy adoption
of a few of my aesthetics
or at least a remembered turn of phrase or two.

Sensible

the future is boiling across the globe
as the youth are getting unruly
with demands for sensible stability
so it's time to ratchet up the social clanks
cordon off the separate ranks
and put them inside fueled up tanks
mix and match the battle flanks
and all the countries agree
it's in their mutual autocratic interests
to slaughter each other's idealists
in organized waves of metalstorms.

Maginot

marianne on the maginot is blowing kisses
and dropping flower petals for germania
paddling down the rhine with her finest parasol
writing love letters in a floral code
from alsace to her dearest lorraine.

Losing A Forever War

the planes take off all day
one after the other in single file
people getting out
brain draining drips until the liberal and secular
and feminist and modern reservoirs are dry
and I put on my veil and close the blinds.

Red Light Mariupol

goddamn it I say
fuck my life
the green light turned to yellow
too far away to make it
and I have to sit at the red light
while the radio news cuts back from its commercial break
and announces the bombing and utter leveling
of several mariupol neighborhoods in the latest history page.

Life For Country

decoy skulls and helmets held above the trench line
get blown to bits by sniping enemy guns
across a field of artillery craters
but the whistles all sound and over we go
it is our turn
orders to the top from the top
and we must ascend
stand tall and run
and shower them with bullets
and sprint like the dickens underneath
before they can lift their heads
from below our volleys of metal
and I force my way to their trench
and shoot them all clear
and I look for my comrades
over my shoulder as I dive inside
but there are none alongside me
I made it alone
and I hear foreign phrases around the ditch curve
and they discover me and raise their rifles
and I raise my hands
to surrender my war
but they pull their triggers
and the bullets spiral
and everything turns slow
closer and closer
bigger and bigger
and they're right between my eyes
and I tighten my brow to take them head on
and that was the war for me.

The Merger Of Church And State

the self-employed prophets talk about god
like they know what he orders at the dive bar corner table
if he prefers a fizzy highball or straight kentucky burn
and the dictators pretend they can hear god's jokes
and slap their knees with demagogic laughs
and these regalia antiquarians and uniform medal collectors
prance ahead of the marching nationalism parade promising
salvation for everyone who suffers for the state
an incredible afterlife wage in an unconvincing mint
but for now here's a sack of flour and bag of beans per family
and pamphlets on the moral satisfaction of tightened belts
and an armband you'll be punished for leaving at home.

Difficult Stump

the forest nymphs came together and danced
joining arms and harmonizing hymns
in a little clearing of their wooded miles
blessing the folk of the open land
with fairy magic charms and generous potlucks
and magnanimous flutist solos conducted by the timber prince
to impress his empress of the bacchanal
and celebrate his subjects of the peaceful wood
but someone told of their pixie mirth
and rapacious village tycoons with hands black from factory soot
scheduled their motors and blades upon the devoted acres
penciling in spreadsheets their estimates of industrial profits
and such was the end of the enchanted wood
save for a deep difficult stump in the middle.

Illicit Shih Tzu

there's a little illicit shih tzu
in campus west housing
who has been living room hot-boxed high more often
than most college students
sprawled out on the floor
in the middle of the peace pipe circle
legs like the breaststroke
stoned out of his simple little doggy mind.

Chat Roulette

basements are always where it happens
guitars going
get sweaty with it
and take a break in front of the oscillating fan
and we agree there's a public show in us
so we turn on the computer cam
and play our guitars in concert building layer upon layer
and amidst the omnipresent masturbators
occasionally a clothed person will watch and smile for a while
but more often all we get
is a hand momentarily letting go of a semi-erect penis
to give a thumbs up before hitting the roulette button
for someone else to masturbate in front of.

Sideboob

looking through her instagram photo batch memories
she thought she couldn't blame the men who ogled her
since she chose such cute outfits always going out
and posted so many photos picking the ones
with ample views down her shirts
and angles of sideboob every chance she got
and bought several new bikini tops every vacation
with pictures of them all a new one each day
on her profile kept public with a dozen tags typed on each
to fully maximize the number of anonymous people
seeing her in their search bar selections and okay she thinks
it's fair not to judge the wandering eyes
cause she looks good and knows it
and goes quite inconveniently out of her way to flaunt it.

manly artist move: write a movie
save money to do it right and direct it to your aesthete taste
cast yourself as the lead
and your number one romantic crush as your protagonist's cinelover
in a critics' choice hit that earns her an oscar
for best actress and makes her rich
as an audition for then asking her out on a date.

The Patriot

he would not fight for his country in war
but he'd patriotically drink and yell and blaspheme
and fight and eat and sloth and love the lonely girls
and otherwise give the boys fighting across the sea
the satisfaction of dying for his freedom at home.

Voyeuristics

he sat in the sun at a red light and then another down the road
and several more while someone crooned vowely syllables slowly on the radio
and the girl in the car behind him was picking her nose for several of them
and he wondered if her ancestors were watching her now
to see what their survival to reproductive age
and gene matching and children raising had led to
this moment of her nose picking
and then wondered if his ancestors were watching him now
sitting bored and hot in traffic
turning pink on the side of his neck
or if they had been watching him earlier jerk off
to a mindless series of videos that led ultimately
to women fluidly debasing themselves for money
and wondered if those women's ancestors had watched them film it
and wondered what would be the point
for anyone's ancestors to sit and watch their progeny
alternatingly bored and unimpressed
and disgusted and disappointed
and even affronted and ashamed
and he wondered if before his birth somehow
he had watched his ancestors' monotonies and degradations
and flaws and sins and wickedness
and he supposed no one's ancestors ever must be watching
since one-way voyeurism wouldn't be fair
and two-way voyeurism of everyone watching everyone else...
what a mess.

this protagonist has no clear goal
his mind is unrealistic and unfocused
and he's on his way to moral failure.

The Stranger

who hasn't been a stranger walking on the beach
under a homicidal taunting algerian sun hissing
'adversus solem ne loquitor'
assaulting every bare foot in the sand and blinding your eyes
to the benign motives in your surf-side stroll
so you accept with open palms the tortured ultimatum
next to arrive for a reprieve finally and definitively from the throng
of empty masks around you on desultory walks to death
muttering their cabalistic incantations of insignificance
clinging to concocted shadows to hide from the inevitable end
and still the sun burns reddening bubbles till they burst
and when the monochrome tunnel vision recedes
and you're seeing colors once again
there's a ribcage ricochet ringing in your ears
and the enemy of your friend is lying in the sand?
who hasn't surrendered to solar savagery
like a cat stretched out across sun stripes on the floor
digging claws into your feet as you step over
when the burn buries too deep into its fur?
feline instinct is all the proof the jury needs
if it mattered what they'd decide
because the absurd has been stalking me close behind
since the sweaty day of the funeral some weeks prior
when I sealed my guilty verdict in its envelope
with tearless cheeks as I poured a cup of coffee
and sipped it slowly thinking of other things
biting into the styrofoam all around the rim
sinking my teeth in memorial to the dragging drowsy hour
while my mother's casket lowered into the ground
and the most regrettable part of all this tribunal drudgery
of the court proceedings and the stone jail cell walls
and the priest babbling on about made up things and wasted prayers
and the guillotine's blade raised above my head
is that the coffee hadn't even been warm.

Natural Apathy

two flies in my room all day
and at night I find them again one on the wall
the other on the window pane
unable to understand why it cannot escape
with no evolutionary explanation for the transparent barrier
and they hang on too weak to fly
and they wait but there's no hope for them
I will not rescue them in a cup and toss them outside
my reason is only laziness
I do not want to get up
so they wait for death
and I forget about them and eventually leave the room
and I go to sleep
and find their bodies
the next time I am in a cleaning mood.

Live In The Moment

stop glorifying the mundanities of your life
you slave to instant gratification
you notification dope fiend
you influenced follower
you amateur paparazzi
you museless narcissist
you avatar sellout
you aesthete of lackluster
you epiphany of mediocrity
you magnificent superfluity
you do not deserve the people's attention.

It's Chill She Says

it's chill she says but it's not
she does her part for the social contract
she is a calm loyal friend
a soothing force on dramatics and they know it
compliment her on it
tell her they wish they were just like her
but still they cannot hold up their half of the bridge
of clammy perfunctory socialite deals.
it's chill she says
because they were going to burn her anyway
because they can't help themselves and their I'm-sorries
are lifeless ocean waves lathering her feet
a swampy salt she smells in silence
smiling the next time she goes out
as the corners of her lips vengefully flirt with their guilt
discernible a fraction of an embarrassed second
before millennial hubris holds their heads
against its breast and absolves them
of their entitled self-centeredness
then they forget but she remembers
cause it wasn't chill.

Calvin & Susie

she looked at me and said
"wait until god hears about this"
and I hit her with the dodgeball
as hard as I could anyway.

RSVP In LA

no one rsvp'ed to the house party
smoke breaking on the boulevard balcony
telling stories loosely based in fact
and everyone would leave
if something else were to come along more fashionably
and some hook up tonight but don't latch on too tight
and are gone in the morning
it's all in the generational clause
with cluttered legalese crafted in texts
of carefully phrased non-commitment
and great-to-see-you hugs looking over shoulders
at who else has shown up
our friendship cannot be owned or counted on
it is licensed only with restrictions applying
we are too cool we followers of social sisyphus
trying so hard and getting nowhere original.

Sainthood

certainly our medieval peasant saints had a host of selfish vices
and moments of violently marvelous malevolent fun.
I can't wait till my moments of unfairness are forgotten
like diamond rings dropped somewhere in miles of beach sand
and my buried ill-mannered interactions
are erased from memory and the record
and my deeds of assistance are sanded from the years
from vaguely impressive to impressively vague
and the myth grows populating moral books and fables
and everyone eventually unknowledgably agrees
I couldn't of course have ever sinned.

Retiring Is For The Dead

the 86-year-old professor hobbles to class
seven minutes late
the back of his shirt already untucked
from the crooked maneuvers necessary to escape his car
the class is waiting sympathetically
as they did every day
and he begins his rhetorical questions
his students can never tell if he wants answered.
the professor speaks slowly
his fifteen-week course could be covered in two by a greener teacher
without the cultural references to long expired decades
and lingering spans of opaque nostalgia
and after ten minutes of rambling
about dead film stars from the movies of his youth
all of which he said last class
he starts the black and white film on vhs tape
and struggles with the missing volume to no avail.
he calls the building's technical help desk.
we wait for the assistant to come
and politely guide him through the process
the professor simply needed to be logged in on his computer
for the audio to play through the speakers
and finally the film begins and the professor shuffles
inch by inch in front of the projection screen
while the video plays across his untucked shirt
and sits down in the front row undulating like a dolphin
to coax his spine into cooperation.
the clock reaches 9:50 and the students leave
the next block is the professor's planning hour
time he uses to finish signing paperwork
regarding teaching another year the coming fall.

Rapport

the old man got in the cab slowly outside the hospital
helped by a nurse into the passenger seat
in which he strategically fell and lifted his legs up inside
as the nurse nestled his oxygen tank by his feet
and tucked in the catheter bag carefully
and then the ride got going
and he struck up light conversation with the driver
to get a bit familiar and build up some rapport
before the ride was up and he'd have to ask
for help carrying into his home his bag of urine.

Polar Bear Plunge

lingering as the floating island drifts
your world is melting
the planet isn't yours anymore
you survey the thawing decay
there's nothing else to do
except anticipate extinction
as your patch dissolves into glacial sea.

Ready

tubes down your throat is a lot for a ninety-year-old lady
and you said not again
you outlived two men the first by too much
but you've had much more happiness than sadness
and above all you are ready.

The 90s Are Over

a lady at my high school graduation gave a lovely speech
that our generation was star-crossed
that we'd have less money than our parents
would live shorter more miserable lives
and the only thing we could do from here on out
is pray that the monodeity pities us
and will someday get bored inflicting this despair
and we booed her and our parents got upset.

do yourself a favor
and come to the realization
your parents were not perfect
and never could be
they were growing up too
and it was understandably childish of you
to expect otherwise.

Company Man

the shop dog kept watch for years
wagging his tail at the passersby
inviting them to take a step inside
and consider the merchandise in stock
and he spied for shoplifters ready to bark
as the boss owners provided him his needs
for being a loyal company man
and kept him on the payroll even after retired and blind
sleeping in the corner sniffing customer shoes
with a pension of petting and hourly treats.

Eons Of Old

you can only truly understand in any profound way
those who are your contemporaries
and you might think unnatural long life a blessing
but it is instead a curse and death itself the blessing
relieving you from living past your era
as your childhood slowly vanishes
and even you can't remember the names or places
just oddly enduring advertising jingles from decades ago
from companies no longer in business
and your values and norms and manners and traditions
have been abandoned by the culture's mercury
and now your profundities bore the young
as you join the ranks of eons of old
complaining about the kids these days
listing to anyone who'll listen all the things
they do of which you don't approve.

Not Your Weird

modernity will pass us all but if you keep an open mind
you won't get upset at getting old
and will even enjoy waving a smiling good day
to all the young weirdos wearing weird fashions
saying weird slang referencing weird new trends and fads
while they do their weird hobbies
to build their weird social reputations for their weird friends
and live out the next generation the way they want
reasonably unconcerned how the generations before feel about it.

Francis Park

charles howard sat on this bench every evening
upon his return from work to smoke a four dollar cigar
he skipped dessert at lunch to buy
for one last moment of peace and calm
between the work of his firm and the work of his sperm
he knew which was more work
seven kids three boys and four girls
so these cigar breaks were guilty pleasures
because the longer he took the closer they all were to bed
while his saintly wife cleaned the dishes and washed the kids
and he told her the cigars were necessary
for boys' club proximity to the boss after business hours
where the real corporate dealing and ladder climbing took place
and he never admitted his puffs were two blocks down from home
but he also was the only man at the firm
he reasoned with himself when calculating sins
without another woman secretly on the side.

a fly of guilt crawled inside my skull
bouncing on the walls of bone confined
and for the rest of my impeccably behaved years
I heard that damn fly buzzing around.

chinese beauty lies in introverted calms
like oriole songs in willow trees along the lake
or a moon glowing self-portraits in an island pond
or pagoda silhouettes in suns setting behind mountains
observing without any disturbances from my western narcissism.

Swim Practice Morning

writing uphill for a week or two
and then finally down a slope
is like a dive into a pool on a sunday morning
in a tight streamline underwater
through dawn's light streaks cutting through the blue
from windows high up in the roof
holding your breath and curving up with the shallow end
blowing bubbles as slow as you can out your nose
head in the grooves of your shoulders and biceps
stretching all the body tendons
from fingertips through the arms and lats
and down the spine to the waist
dolphin kicking slowly and powerfully
till your fingertips poke the concrete wall at the other end
that keeps you from escaping into the sea
joining a galavanting pod out in the blue
and eating mackerel every day for lunch.

so many wonderful cultures on this planet
into which I regrettably will never get to assimilate.

I went to the bathroom two hours ago
before the presentation of my proposal
to the executives sans lectern
just a lot of open space in the back of the room
to explain powerpoints on a screen
of a career advancing strategy certain to impress them all
and I just found my fly undone.

homo sapiens have this weird tendency
to become wildly obsessed with various hobbies
and schemes of recreation with such gusto
that the gravity of conversations at dinner party tables
is sucked inward where no other subjects can escape
not unlike the blackhole at the center of our galaxy.

Cash Only

in the shady car inspection place
cause her car maybe wouldn't pass an honest emissions test
the calendar pages are brown and hard
from dried spills and cigarette ash
and the desk man says he's tired to his friend
"I spent the weekend at the lake
and man the young pussy wears me out
I always think I can take it but I can't
and I'm a baby daddy already with that bitch anyway
I told her I didn't want anything to do with her before the kid
but if the kid needed anything I'd take care of it
but I wasn't gonna pay no monthly alimony
and I already got a bond over a bogus claim
from her other baby daddy cause he's getting jealous
saying he can send me back to jail
but he ain't got nothing on me
cause I never leave saint louis
I don't ever play or nothing east side anymore
those warrants can't get me
oh by the way"
he turns to her
"we take cash only."

Mayor Of Enlightenment

I found a disgruntled bodhisattva in a pool hall angry
cause he missed a shot and scratched
and plopped the eight in a pocket he didn't call
and lost a lot of money
and he told me he quit
and nominated me the next local mayor of enlightenment
and said it's easy to fake it
all you gotta do is riddle up a fact
or ask expectant pilgrims nonsensical things like
when is the rain most wet?
and if that doesn't send them away
tell them to cut out all their dualities
and only monoize from here on out
and that will do the trick to get them off and thinking
though most importantly away from you
because he said
this you'll find early and eternal
the desperate for awakening are very clingy.

when I get a cold I don't rest
or sleep it off or stay in at night
I stalk it with whiskey and red wine and tank tops
and harass it with weight lifting in my living room
and a jogging architectural tour on swift feet outside
to not just break the siege of antagonistic bacteria
but spear their nuclei on stakes
as a reminder of what happens
when espionage is committed against my iron bloodstream.

Bloodbath

elizabeth báthory soaking in a bloodbath takes sips
of her epileptic tonic cure but tomorrow she'll still have seizures
and will need a few more maidens from the countryside.

DyNasty

the royal heredity was a web of sexual politics
enticing incest with familial intrigue
and the sisters-in-law tempted all the husbands
and everyone eyed their cousins for broom closet gasps
and the stately princes were raised apart from the peasant masses
with delusions of grandeur delivering them from their divine wombs
and the family tree was closely pruned
and the aunts and the uncles and the brothers and the sisters
mixed and matched the family jewels
till the familial branches got themselves tied up
with knotty fruits of ugly sociopaths for generations in a row
and the monarchies deformed and lost grasp of reality
and the enlightened peoples of the continent agreed
the royal heads were better unattached.

death himself must be tired
of the long lines of lives he must take
are his arms sore from swinging his scythe
does he ever slip on a puddle of blood and take a hiatus
does the reaper like to be relieved of his work
and take off his robe and sleep on a beach sometimes
or does he bring his work along
snorkeling underwater nicking feet of floating vacationers
and then go swimming with the sharks?

Halloween Is My Favorite Time Of The Year

my dreams are of dismembered hands
and emulsified jars of bloodied hearts
and I lurk about the streets
where no one perceives my serial killing instincts
or hears the piercing screams echoing endlessly in my head
halloween is my favorite time of year
because I fit right in with all the holiday spookery
and no one knows that I'm not bluffing.

The Apartment Turnover

there's a skull in the wall
its mandible and cheek bones are right there
stretching out a couple layers of paint
I believe the landlord has painted over the former tenant.

Gonna Get Weird

maybe it's the spider bite in my thigh
growing volcanically and getting hot
or the thunderstorm outside flashing lightning like a rave
or the dust-scrape bowl I am smoking
or the edible just starting to hit
or the bottle of discount grain alcohol I just finished
but I feel like tonight is gonna get weird.

Beside Me Behind The Podium

allow me to publicly apologize to my liver
for the harm and pain I caused it last night
after drinking a power-hour sprinkled with shots of gin
merely for performative bravado amongst my peers
I regret my actions
and accept all responsibility for
and consequences from them
and I can only hope
though I note it is quite undeserved
that my liver will continue to support me
throughout all my future endeavors.
forever yours
dash.

The Hand-Off

with a wink to the mexican and a handshake eye to eye
he hands me the bag and I hand him the money
and he walks back inside
and I get on the transit train and can't wait
I open up the bag and smell it
damn it's potent stuff
and start eating
it's the best burrito I've ever had
I tipped five dollars on the order online
and must have gotten double the steak as usual.

Cessna Noon

the week day shifts pass slow but the weeks sprint swift
and the months have yet more haste
as my youth dissolves in the daily poison shake
of blue collar work only drinking helps forget and erase
from consideration the thousands of days I've already used up
so I pound a beer
order shots for the after-work crew and start beer two
and accept the favor returns so in twenty-five minutes
I am veritably tanked and the night is an infant still
but its remainder is black next morning shipwreck washed up
on cracked banks of dried up memory seas
and my stomach must be resuscitated slowly
writhing around in thin bedsheets and empty bottles of rum
while slowly the cessna noon floats overhead and stalls
as my headache lashes out to secure its coup d'état
ordering me up on my feet to dress for work.

everything finite is magnificent
the gods watch us
not us them.

The Diner Swivel

the diner doors open
and the old men sitting at the counter
in the seats they always take
turn their bodies in the swivel chairs
and look at who is coming in.

Awning

the rain keeps me under
the awning of a coffee shop.

my coffee's all gone
but the rain won't stop.

nothing to do
but order another.

Last Of His Sixties' Red

an old man in a cafe with a white mustache
tinged with the last of his sixties' red
turned pages of his newspaper
and tapped cigarettes on his mug into the coffee mud
as stray ashes fell on words dispatching world events
soon to be carrying on without him
and he watched the young tourist girls walk by his taverna
toward the island's iconic ruins and beaches dressed for travel selfies
and he marveled at their fashions
and the curves the girls were generous in showing off
and he thought of the girls of his generation and their spunk
such conservative fashion these years later but revolutionary then
and he admired the independence successes
of women advancing through the decades
against the constructed fortifications of his own sex
in every field of liberty and thought and talent
and gorgeous self-expression
and he thought about each pretty lady passing
one after another thinking to himself
good for you girl
good for you.

Where The Buck Stops

three generations in a row on the train
and the little girl on the end has her imagination at work
with a winged princess doll
wrapping her birthstone necklace around the wings
and spinning it around
but the princess quickly gets caught up in the chain
and she can't untangle it so frustratedly hands it to her right
to her mother who takes a go at it
and is quickly frustrated as well
and hands it to her right to her mother who works at it diligently
the family's buck stops with her
and she frees the princess and hands it back down the line
and the girl's imagination gets back to work.

Little Duckling

a little duckling in hangzhou's west lake
alone among the lotus flowers
dips down suddenly and is gone
and his ripples spread out and thin
and the water calms to glass
and still he's under...
I worry if he's okay
did he get eaten by a large carp?
several seconds of concern go by
but several yards away
his head pops up and he chirps a note
and shakes his head
and down under he goes again.

Odyssey Hearts

the doors are open for the travelers from across the world
to dance out on the stone mykonos steps
leading into the calm aegean edge between lit patio candles
looking out at reflections of nightclub lights flickering
spinning color theories of electric flashing lasers
beaming in the sea to share the fun with dolphins and octopi
as the travelers share their odyssey hearts
and music and wine in the trancing harbor
hypnotized by cycladic muses caressing the crowd
until they wake up at noon the day that follows
with groggy happy memories and a faint headache
that just needs a little something fresh to eat.

Santorini

I spilled out of a bag of marbles
and rolled the furthest of the cyclades
then cracked across the middle blowing up big
wrecking havoc all about
and they think my cliffs are pretty
and pour cement and paint it all white
and come with camera things and engagement rings
but I'm not yet done with my bursting
still got lava in my magma veins
and they're really taking a chance
coming to my volcano top.

Souvenir Gambling

is there anything more disappointing than perusing souvenir shops
and noticing a statue or vase or trinket you like
and buying it satisfied to display on your library shelf
and then immediately finding in the next store
the same item for several euros cheaper?
at least it won't be long before you are a little relieved
when you see it more expensive in a third or fourth shop
and you can smile at least
that you didn't get the very worst deal.

Bombing

a little conversation with a new acquaintance
did not go as well as others regularly do and oh well
won't be seeing them again anyway
but it's a nagging bother and won't let go
and stays there in my head
the things I said and the things I should have said
and the things I definitely should not have said
my impulses calibrated incorrectly
for an audience not in a receptive mood
to hear my interjections and obscure references
and I misread the room and bombed
and the audience's silence still lingers in the painful air.

you're never more than a couple hours away
from making something creative and interesting and neat.

Free Content For The Masses

she makes free content for the masses
and of course to start it will quickly be done
and suffer a tad for quantity over precision of agonized quality
while her aesthetic taste remains a bit beyond
her early talent and initial artistic executions
but they have no right to complain
as she offers it all for free on her digital notebooks
so she suffers no guilt and is not compelled to stop and argue
instead keeping a monkish code of dedicated focus
to preserve with her strengthening hands and emitting mind
as many epiphanies as can be cranked out
to build her audience and follower count
and portfolio of completed canvas dazzles
for the benefit of the zeitgeist and for future generations
to remember and hopefully commercialize her
in cheap pop fashions in future discount retail stores
so she'll live forever in a canon niche she created all herself
all because in the now
she is brightening and widening her evolving skylight signal
glowing in the words of mouth of sharing influencers
one publishing at a time.

quite extremely confident humility is a burden on patience
when people try to blow up your ego with ignorant admiration
for a work badly executed that you've regrettably ruined
and to dislike when others exclaim their poor taste
with words of banal encouragement or other unearned awards
is the mark you're on your way
to some form of artistic individuality.

Art Blurb

an expansive collection of statements
on the ephemeral nature of the human condition
juxtaposing well-traveled anecdotes with literary and philosophical muses
in a page-turning cacophony of metaphysical speculations
hallmarked with a neo-retro-post-modernist's insatiable anxiety
reconfiguring with subtle form the dimensional depths
of readers' latent delusions into a contemporary synesthete manifesto
on the dangers of our generation's hubristic lust for decadence
this work is a pyrrhic triumph amidst our shrinking attention spans
a diligent epitaph for the hegemonic deconstructive dynamics
of the 2010s and 2020s decades' hypocritical absurdities
ubiquitous in our ascendant cultural identity civil warring
with brave bold criticism of the digital ramifications
of our transactional and hustle culture millennial ideals and angsts.
3.8/5

One-Hit Wonder

he was a filmmaker with real depth
making pennies from his craft for years
until a lackadaisical project mocking pop consumerism
turned ironically viral and found eyes of the famous
and suddenly he was flush with riches and testimonials
and his showings and premiers were fabulous affairs
for the cultural elites who had no erudite taste
just drank their cocktails in the theatre lobby
hobnobbing with the rest of the meretricious bourgeoisie
who never actually watched his films.

South City, Saint Louis

I woke up and showered
dressed business casual with tall colorful socks
stepped across the living room
to the wooden corner desk by the open window
and did my day of business.
the breeze picked up a little after noon
and the brewery air wafted southwest
and I got drunk off the malted breeze
and the whiskey I was sipping
and the words I was writing.

I very often find myself with feelings of heartfelt gratitude
that my infant eyes opened and looked down to examine
the feeble limbs of a holocene hominid.

Futurist

noon stares at the boulevard
its horses pulling carriages prancing down below the balcony
as I sip a drink of rye and puff at a cigar
while an ice delivery is paid for downstairs
so I can be brought a chunk of it
and chisel off a shard into the tumbler glass and stir
light up again my cigar
and contemplate my regret of not being born
in a more convenient era.

The Flâneur's Day Off

good morning in the gold
on the couch against the window
the boulevard is calm
and so am I.

Positivity Governs

on a cafe's sidewalk patio chair
a girl sits alone at the table next to mine
talking loudly on the phone
about a promotion and a raise...
how positive life can sometimes be.

Happiness Masterpieces

your soul is in your crow's feet
the wrinkles in your eyes when you smile
are you a happy person
do you laugh a lot
are you really laughing now
are you really happy?

Adeline Ravoux

he painted her sitting in the inn and said to keep still
but she kept turning her head to see how he did it
to try and see like how he saw.

Impressionist

I've written so many poems yet covered so few
of all the profound thoughts and moments
I've had the privilege or misfortune to meet
art can never keep up with life
but it would be uninteresting and cheap if it could.

Back To Hannibal

he wandered about his old hometown streets
seeing familiar faces on the little girls
the daughters of the ladies he used to love.

full san francisco moon over chinatown in winter
where the poet sits
and eats cheap lo mein on the street curb.

there is no greater trophy
than a fully read book sitting on your bookshelf.

Dash MacIntyre has been writing poetry since his college years, and this is a collection of some of his poems spanning the last decade from these chapbooks:

Window Lamp	(2010-2012)
Porch Couch	(2012-2014)
Rooftop Toasts	(2015-2016)
Odd Hours	(2016-2017)
Expatriate	(2018-2019)
Mt. Monastic	(2019-2020)
The Conversateur	(2020-2022)

MacIntyre is also the creator of **The Halfway Post**, a digital newspaper of Dadaist graffiti news and satirical comedy that daily makes fun of Donald Trump.

Besides *THP*, MacIntyre has published comedy lots of places, including *McSweeney's Internet Tendency*, *Points In Case*, *Little Old Lady*, *MuddyUm*, and *The Haven*.

To keep up with MacIntyre's daily writing studio, subscribe to his *Substack* newsletter **The Halfway Café**.

DASH MACINTYRE'S BOOKS

POETRY
Cabaret No Stare (2022)
Moon Goon (2023)
Hotel Golden Hours (2024)

POLITICAL SATIRE
Satire In The Trump Years: The Best Of The Halfway Post (2021)
Satire In The Biden Years: The Worst Of The Halfway Post (2025)

Like my writing? Subscribe to my Substack!

TheHalfwayCafe.Substack.com
Linktr.ee/DashMacIntyre

www.ingramcontent.com/pod-product-compliance
Lightning Source LLC
Chambersburg PA
CBHW020948090426
42736CB00010B/1325